WOMAN IN A BLUE ROBE

By the Same Author

Epitaph for Memories (The Bunny and the Crocodile, 2002)
trilogy & Hagoromo: A Celestial Robe (Ikuta, 2010)
Aquamarine (Glass Lyre, 2014)

WITH JAMES C. HOPKINS
The Blue Door (Word Works, 2006)

WITH JAMES C. HOPKINS & BERNARD STOLZ
a sleeping tiger dreams of manhattan: poetry, photographs and sound
(Ikuta, 2008)

AS TRANSLATOR
Songs and Stories of the Kojiki (Ahadada, 2008;
2nd, revised edition, Red Moon, 2014)

Woman in a Blue Robe

Yoko Danno

ISOBAR PRESS

First published in 2016 by

Isobar Press
Sakura 2-21-23-202, Setagaya-ku,
Tokyo 156-0053, Japan

&

14 Isokon Flats, Lawn Road,
London NW3 2XD, United Kingdom

http://isobarpress.com

ISBN 978-4-907359-16-4

© Yoko Danno, 2016

All rights reserved.

Acknowledgements appear on page 65.

Contents

I

Last Supper	11
Evolution	12
Alchemy Lesson	13
Germination	14
Snow Adventure	15
What Have You Seen?	16
Narrow Path	17
Flower Passages	19
Tea Ceremony House	21
Offering to the Blue Sky	22

II

Squid Ink	25

III

in the fountain	30
In Pursuit of a Bird	31
Wild Nights	33
Dream of a Butterfly	35
Linked Verse with Saigyō	37
Sleeping Tiger	38
Flower Arrangement	41
Spring of Life	43

Herb Tea Time	45
Missing Piece of the Puzzle	47
Hide-and-Seek	49
Serpent, Tornado	51
Renovation	53
Woman in a Blue Robe	55
Sole Desire	57
Notes & Acknowledgements	63

for my granddaughters

Sakino & Yasuha

I

Last Supper

After traveling
through thousands of years
starlight touches

the only persimmon
left luminous
at the treetop,

the last supper
for birds
going home

into
the sunset

Evolution

On a cave wall are painted
scenes of bison
being hunted,

of humans
killing their fellow
Homo sapiens,

on TV screens
scenes
of squeezing

juice
out of all sentient
brains

Alchemy Lesson

At the College of Magical Arts
when I was young, the first lesson
was to change fire
into water,

then
rock into
violet quartz,

the ultimate aim
being, as you know,
to change base metal
into gold –

but mind you,

there's always a critical
turning point – I've heard of one
who transformed himself
into a rain of gold

to make love,

and also
of a city burnt
in a flash of light,

a mushroom
cloud
turning

into black rain

Germination

Where was I
before I was inside you?

Was I blowing
like a wind across the sky,
slipping through a cloud of birds?

You were there in the seed, dear

Is that why I was named Yoko, 'Leaf-Child'?

A welcome rain
falls on the mountains
changes into

quick-crystal streams,
glancing through rocks,

growing and glowing, sweet
lovers
of the mother

earth

Snow Adventure

By midday, warmed
by the piercing sunshine,

trees shed heaps
of snow from their limbs

as if slipping out
of padded
white kimonos,

stand naked
in the slanting rays
like antennas,

ready
for communication

with meteors

What Have You Seen?

They say mountains,
trees and flowers
don't travel,

but I have seen
a mountain walk
into the sea,

trees move
to the other side
of a rain forest,

an alpine plant
resign its seat
to another

so that the other
may survive

at such altitude

Narrow Path

the
dried-
up
path
is
lead-
ing
to
a
shim-
mery
lake
far
ahead;

across
burn-
ing
hills
we
weave
through

grey
wavering
grasses

until we come to –

a place where

    two-humped
   camels blare
  like sirens,
   flushing
   a flock
    of desert
     birds
    from
   the lush
oasis,

  where
 we steep
  our feet
    in the darkly
    seeping
     pure

     water

Flower Passages

1

Wisteria
flowers
almost
touching
the ground,
I knit
a pullover
for my lover,
the yarn
not long enough
to complete
the fancy pattern

2

Lingering in my overgrown garden,
I find thistles to my taste, dry nettles not.

Pears resemble avocados only in shape:
I realize I have no idea what on earth I am.

3

Workmen are digging beside a sasanqua
hedge. 'Why is this needed here?'
'To carry fallen petals to the sewer –
to keep your words flowing…'

4

A black swallowtail fluttering
    from a mist of orange blossoms
leads me to an empty hallway:
    through a crack in the closed door
a shaft of sunlight pierces the dark.

Tea Ceremony House

The way to your destination
is not simple – after getting off
the train at the suburban station,

cross the railroad to the opposite
side, walk along the street flanked
with prefabricated modern houses,

turn into a narrow bypath a car can
barely pass through; a wooden mansion,
generations old, looms ahead – the main

gate that once admitted noblemen on
horseback is fastened now with a bar.
Inside the wall by way of the side door,

tips of rock islands rise above the sea
of white pebbles mixed with fallen
flower petals – watered stone steps

lead you to the tea ceremony house,
where a weeping cherry tree in full
blossom awaits you – a swift shadow

of a huge bird passes across the empty
pool – before the spring storm hits you,

      please drink

   this peaceful tea

Offering to the Blue Sky

Clockwise
    I turn three times
        bowl of green tea on my palm
            an offering to the clear blue sky

        Up on the high plateau
      people and yaks
    circumambulate
      the snow-capped
        sacred mountain

Go around,
    mawatte, mawatte, mawatte,
        life is a rotating dream

Afraid of fallout
    I cover the bowl
        with a hydrangea leaf

II

Squid Ink

one of a thousand flowery goldfish,
fluttering in a huge LED-lit glass bowl,
my voice silently rising as tiny bubbles

*

shaggy peaks shine before sunset,
lava erupts from a crack of a smile

*

a word is a tool
that shapes bloody sea fish
into exquisite *sashimi*

*

a slave of words, in sorrow or delight,
sole resident in a mushroom of a house,
attending sincerely on my 'chronic disease'

*

sunlit maple trees burst into red and yellow
preparing for loneliness in deep snow
and the approach of silence below zero

*

wind beats against the window
dim light leaks through a gap in the cloud
the full harvest moon is nowhere in sight

*

in the deep sea squids targeting fish
always win the game; in love they go
into close rapport with their mates
without any use of ink, ichthyologists say

*

staring into a crystal ball is of no avail
in looking for hair-pins or the future

*

Recipe for Tonight

1. a spoonful of madness
2. some kind of bait to lure fish
   or the opposite sex
3. a phosphorescent simile
4. a pinch of secret vice added
   to the chicken broth

*

cups and glasses not wrapped,
clothes still hanging in the wardrobe,
bundles of goods for removal on the floor –
stop falling *sakura*, I'm not yet ready to depart

III

in the fountain is a stone
        in the stone is a crevice
within the crevice is a key
        with the key i open a door
beyond the door is another door
        in a fence around a garden

in the lush garden is a fountain
        reflecting a cloud in the sky
within the cloud is a golden key
        with the key i open another door

behind the door is a green man
        with a bag full of flower seeds
i sow the seeds, which take root
        in the sky reflected in the water

bright yellow flowers come out
        casting light on my bedside table

In Pursuit of a Bird

I feel time flies faster than ever. Because I digest food more slowly of late? Or am I already traveling around another sun, or another star? I hope the orbit of my thought can be traced more precisely and the geography in my brain explored in more detail. Ethereal fragments of consciousness, along with earthbound urges, should be eventually put together into a meaningful whole. Is there a mastermind behind all of this mysterious process of integration?

I sent a letter to my friend at his former address. I didn't know he had moved. Someone told me he has gone in search of a bird. Where?

In pursuit of the swan, he arrived at the land of Harima by way of Ki, then crossing Inaba he came to Tanba and to Tajima. He followed the bird eastward to the land of Ōmi, crossed Mino, chased it through Owari, past Shinano, and finally in the land of Koshi spread a net at a river mouth…

The man in the tale had been told that if he found the bird, the emperor's young son, who was unable to speak, would be cured. But is it possible, at the present time, to wander over the Japanese islands of the eighth century? Let alone to find the bird? I'm told the past is a mirage, the future a phantom, and now becomes past from instant to instant – a flower never stays the same. But then, what is the present time exactly? If there's no now, do we live only in the past? If so, no wonder he has gone looking for the bird in the past – is that what he has been doing while I've been waiting for his reply? Where on earth has he flown to? The one to whom I sent a letter, I mean.

My letter is, I imagine, being carried around in a postman's bag in search of his whereabouts. I hope it won't be abandoned in a box of undelivered mail at a post office, since I forgot to write my return address on the envelope. A fatal fault. Once lost, a letter will never be delivered. To my dismay, I may never find out whether he has actually caught the bird or not, although I desperately wish to know.

I have recently lost my voice, caused not by laryngeal cancer, but by hypertension – I am required to perform magic in front of old people in a nursing home. Most of the audience are suffering from dementia, but I've been warned they are strangely quick-eyed in seeing through tricks. It's rumored they are trained nightly by expert owls to see through the darkness. If only I could regain my voice, I might distract their attention with my hocus pocus.

I wonder, however, if we should always expect replies to our letters. Emily Dickinson wisely stored her letters to her 'Master' in a small casket. Her prudence has kept the world in perpetual suspense and contemplation. Thinking I might perhaps have forgotten to mail my letter, I rummaged all drawers of my desk and cabinet – in vain. There's no doubt that I posted it – *or is the letter still in my brain?*

Wild Nights

I wanted to prolong my stay downstairs a little longer so that she might be finished for good in the bathtub upstairs. But instead I ran up the stairs to pull her out of the water – just in time – while she was still alive. Who was the drowning woman? My indispensable other – a flagpole to fasten my tightrope to?

I had been struggling for days without success to write a poem about this woman. She appears in the mirror on the wall from time to time when I look at my reflection and sets my nerves afire. I just wanted to ask her how she had managed to escape from her cocker spaniel and the Spaniard, who she said were untiringly stalking her.

She's a big woman and is always accompanied by friends, but whenever I try to observe her closely the spaniel and the Spaniard appear and the three of them form an area like the Bermuda Triangle. I usually lose sight of her in the fog of this magical space.

You know, however hard you try to flee from your Spanish giant or your fellow dog, you can't, because they're a part of what you are. If you successfully dismissed them, your whole system would eventually fail – that's my fear. There's no taming one's nature except practice, practice, practice! *The rain in Spain stays mainly in the plain* – whose words?

I feel a current of humid air from the south and hear the calls of birds hurrying home. Cicadas have stopped singing – a sure sign of a storm. Clouds are gathering. They will soon have entirely covered the sky, and there will be no gap through which I might have a chance to peep into a world beyond as vast and deep as a madness for flight. Yes, an easy breakthrough is rare.

It's blowing wildly, sleet bangs on the roof tiles, my old house creaks and trembles. In occasional flashes of lightning a pair of trees are revealed – their boughs intertwined, their trunks joined together like Siamese twins; roars of worries howl across the hill, sending shivers up my spine. Visibility becoming poor. How I wish for a clear night!

Dream of a Butterfly

> *a butterfly perches on my hand –*
> *a few seconds for me,*
> *but an eternity for the insect*

The door bell rang, rang and rang. I reluctantly left my couch and made for the door, as if wading through water. I found nobody outside except a large, black swallowtail fluttering away. I returned to my comfortable chair and took up the book I'd been reading. The pages were blank, all the words gone – and I couldn't even remember exactly what book it was. Was it a work on a learn-while-sleeping method by a famous lepidopterist?

> *a swarm of butterflies flutter*
> *in an illuminated glass-house,*
> *light deflected off their wings*

Out in the field children were chasing pollinators to pin them in insect cabinets – their summer homework. Every time a boy gave a shout of glee, the long grasses trembled like nerve fibers, agitated, restless, as if rubbed the wrong way by the sweep of the net. I was put in a cage with other winged fellows – for eons.

> *struggling to wake, i find myself*
> *among the butterflies in a cage,*
> *my wings tattered like tissue paper*

The door bell rang again, louder and louder. My eyes stopped at the margin of a blank page. A ravine was under my nose, and beyond, an overhanging cliff with a few low pines in the shapes of crouching animals. I was sitting in a chair placed on the grass-covered plateau. Someone was playing a contrabass. The deep sound echoed back like waves of hunger. The breeze smelt salty as if coming from the sea. Somehow I thought of the steamed-rice balls wrapped in thin sheets of dried seaweed which I had stored in the freezer, just in case.

> *the land quakes, cicada nymphs*
> *tremble, the terracotta soldiers*
> *guarding the underground palace*
> *shudder in alarm – attention!*

The air was warm and humid. I strolled among palm trees in the glass-house filled with the perfume of orange and yellow tropical flowers. When I stood still, holding my breath, wishing the moment would last, butterflies came to settle on my shoulders and on my palm, for honey. The bell started ringing again – closing time at the butterfly farm. I had to leave this Shangri-la.

On my way home I stumbled over a stone that had tumbled down the hillside. Yes, I realized, there had been, to be sure, an earthquake.

Linked Verse with Saigyō

Heaped with snow
bamboo in the garden
bend and topple –   (Saigyō)

> *only yesterday the branching river*
> *was young, rushing between rocks*   (Yoko)

Ice wedged fast
in the crevice of the rock
this morning begins to melt –   (Saigyō)

> *fertilized eggs rest under thin ice*
> *ready to be borne to unseen oceans*   (Yoko)

I'll forget the trail…
go seeking for blossoms
in directions I've never seen before   (Saigyō)

> *your unknown features are seen*
> *through your own cast-off skins*   (Yoko)

Even in a person
most times indifferent
to things around him   (Saigyō)

> *a smile escapes from the tight lips*
> *when silver peaks glow at sunset*   (Yoko)

Sleeping Tiger

The Pass of Nakayama was dusky although it was midday. The thick foliage of the tall trees blocked the sunlight. We cut through the woods along an ancient path paved with cobblestones until we came to an open place commanding a view over the waves of tea fields to the north – far in the distance an undulating range of mountains lay in the haze. The breeze felt cool on my sweaty cheeks.

> Did I ever anticipate
> Crossing this pass
> Again in my old age?
>   My life is fulfilled
>   On Mt Nakayama   (Saigyō)

Had I ever breathed the scent of the early summer grass here? Had I followed this gloomy winding road before?

Abruptly an image of a tiger lying among the tea shrubs flashed across my mind, with an odd question: what were you doing when the Bomb was dropped? I had no idea how to answer – then an internal voice began chanting drowsily, 'seeds are stars, stars are seeds,' like fading thunder...

We were just in time for the train across the mainland for the castle town – but rumor had it that the whole town was contaminated by radiation – that a flying saucer... no, a huge fire ball had burst in the air... ever since then the soil itself has been radioactive... no grass has grown, no birds sung, no fish swum in the sparkling clear water...

Did I turn off the gas at the main before we left home? The plugs out of the sockets? The refrigerator cleared?

That was no way our picture of the destination. We had expected fireflies would swirl over the grass, owls hoot in the willow trees, rivers run noisily over singing pebbles, and beneath a blossoming wisteria trellis a pair of empty chairs would be waiting for us…

Did I close the kitchen windows? Are the doors all locked? The burglar alarm on?

I thought our train was bound for the south and the sun. But the sky was suddenly filled with clouds and it started raining…

Did I take the laundry in from the balcony?

The scenery beyond the window began to move forward crazily. The engine driver had put the train into reverse – was rewinding time – so we became younger as we went upstream, following the course of a vast river, laughing like children going home…

We got off the train at a divide where the dust from space was falling on snowy mountains. Columns of ice towered ahead like five shimmering fingers, and an expanse of golden flowers was spread below in the purple light. At the last minute before sunset my mobile phone beeped…

We resumed walking. A little further on, there was a stone monument by the roadside with a Bashō poem inscribed on it –

like some kind of turning point. When I stepped forward to the monument, I felt as if I had crossed a line – an invisible line drawn along the meandering ups and downs of the Path…

> My life is fulfilled
> Cool air flows
> Under my small sedge hat

A bush warbler sang in flight. Time for the dreaming tiger to wake up.

Flower Arrangement

An expanse of rape blossoms –
the moon in the east
the sun in the west

My twin brother and I together carved out a cave in the snow. For two nights and days we stayed in there while a snowstorm raged outside. Our rations were just enough for forty-eight hours. One of us stayed awake while the other slept.

By the morning of the third day the storm had spent itself and the blue sky could be seen through the thin clouds. A lone helicopter was circling above the opposite ridge, breaking the stillness of the cold.

Wading through the fresh snow, I pictured my mother lying in bed in hospital. She looked as if she was sleeping in deep water, but then she surprised me by suddenly surfacing for a breath and opening her eyes. She appeared to be seeing the world for the first time.

She got up and left the sickroom with me. She walked unexpectedly fast for a 93-year old. I couldn't keep up with her. When I came to, in my hand was a black button I had torn from her overcoat. Like a tender spot on my palm.

It gradually dawned on me that it was a button to open and shut the windows of our house. My twin brother, a red rose in his buttonhole, touched the button. A landscape pulsing with purple light spread out before our eyes.

Snow-capped mountains soar like the teeth of a shark, a field of golden rape blossoms wavers in the slanting sun – a pale half moon is rising in the eastern sky.

Spring of Life

The first wind of spring blows from the south. The sunlight streams into my room and I inhale the scent of the narcissi blooming under the window.

Today I have found no vernal messages on my computer screen, no harbingers of spring in my mailbox, no red wine in my crystal-clear glass, but at every street corner I notice a shadow which is just turning left, or right… or just vanishing into the mist of yellow dust.

I decide to follow it. When I reach the corner, however, it has already turned off. I quicken my pace, but by the time I reach the next corner, the shadow has long disappeared. Finally I give up and continue walking until I come to my regular path along the riverside.

The running water appears almost gelatinous in the soft sunlight. As usual I look for the pair of white herons, but they are nowhere to be seen. Perhaps I just want to find a *dokodemo* door – an 'anywhere door', a door to wherever you like. But I can't think of anywhere I'd particularly like to go. Then suddenly a door in my memory springs open. Yes, on that summer day in my childhood, I knew exactly where I wanted to go:

All my older friends had jumped into the water and begun to swim across the river. The water was far deeper than the height of a seven-year old. I had to decide whether to follow them or to return home by myself. I jumped in before thinking further, strongly drawn to the opposite shore where pink flowers were swaying in a breeze. The next thing I knew I was struggling in the water. While kicking frantically, my feet felt a rushing spring and I somehow surfaced. To my surprise I managed to dog-paddle to the other shore. I was happier than I had ever felt in my young life when, thoroughly spent, I lay on my stomach on the sun-warmed pebbles...

I continue walking and come to the mouth of the river and sit on the bank, watching a flock of wild ducks float on the glittering water. The tide is on the ebb, gradually revealing the riverbed. Some of the ducks are plunging their heads into the water for food. Some are preening, some waddling across the sandbank. Clouds start gathering and soon cover the whole sky. The bright colors of the scenery fade by degrees and finally turn into black and white. The ducks are curled up like speckled stones. The leaves of the reeds look long and sharp like knives. Suddenly I realize: yes, this is where I must come to depart from this life.

Herb Tea Time

Sea swallows dive
for fish – wind blows
across the reed-grown shore

Hung high up on the wall of my living room is a framed photo – the profile of a horse, browsing, or smelling the fresh grass, his eye fondly looking down on the tiny yellow flowers at the tip of his nose. The photo my friend gave me as a keepsake of her late husband.

His end at 58 years old came abruptly. You might say there's no end or beginning in time but only the continuous present – a horse browsing the grass, a sweet smell rising from the flowers. The scene freezes – or starts living – when the shutter is released with a click.

One cold morning in midwinter in a park near our house, my baby son suddenly pulled his hand free of my grasp and stood on his own two legs for the first time. He trotted a few steps and fell, got up and resumed his new-found adventure, over and over again. He launched himself forward as if diving for a prize. He looked so determined and alone.

Time lapses: a blur on the seashore, and I'm lost in a warm, soft breeze, in a reverie, out of myself; my son might be my twin brother or a lover, and I, his daughter or a girlfriend, basking together in the sun on the white sands. Laughter wafts through the pine needles, and the sound of bathers one after another diving from a high platform into the sea slightly disturbs the salty air.

He is always smiling in his photos: in his baby bathtub, in a mountain stream in the Japan Alps, or in a hot spring in India. No hint at all of the precipitate fall from a Himalayan peak at the age of 22. It happens in a flash, a fall from a knife-edge ridge, or from a horse. But whether you've lived through many summers or not makes no difference to the delight of smiling in a hot spring, of smelling flowers or of sipping tea.

Herb leaves are steeping in the hot water – the aroma is rising…

Missing Piece of the Puzzle

> *Praise to the horse-headed Kannon, Hayagrīva!*
> *The goddess of mercy with three wrathful faces!*

For a week my sister wouldn't talk to me because I was two hours late for an appointment. My daughter blamed me because I had planted cucumbers instead of pansies in her flower garden. My husband blew his top because I reproached him for having lost a piece of my jigsaw puzzle. A silly accusation – actually I had lost it. Ashamed of myself, I grasped a kitchen knife tightly. I had nothing to hold onto within reach.

I dashed out of the house like a racehorse, repeating in my mind, 'Once the connection between man and horse is broken, the heart skips a beat, and the fence to be cleared looms high.' I ran on, heading for the mouth of the river so that I could let all my sins and worries flow away along with my shoes and clothes and underwear – just like our ancient people would have done in a purification ritual.

Later I returned to the house. A breeze was streaming in through the kitchen window. The homeless cat came punctually to his favorite spot in the shade of a full-blown azalea and lay down. The living picture beyond the window frame was given a bright finishing touch when the sun came out from behind the clouds. I was cutting chives to make noodle soup for lunch. I began to feel uneasy when I realized I had not felt this kind of perfection for a long time.

If only I could find the missing piece of my jigsaw. Would the world be changed? Would the once-hurt harmonious whole be restored? I have cut chives a thousand times in my life. I have watched the clouds break and reveal the sun; it's nothing out of the ordinary. I have often seen the stray cat sitting under a blossoming tree. But I have never before experienced perfect harmony – a harmony on the verge of falling apart with the smallest of actions.

'Keep your wound open,' a lama once said. 'How can you feel the faintest breeze if a scab has formed over it?' Wishing to sustain the precarious moment as long as possible, I froze. The breeze dropped. The breathless silence was broken by the shrill call of a butcher-bird. The cat rose and bristled. Feeling in some way relieved, I resumed cutting chives with an approving smile. A thin cloud brushed over the sun.

Hide-and-Seek

In the drawer of my family altar
is another world –

The fall was sudden. I was tossed up in the air and didn't know where I was until I crashed onto the ground. My horse, frightened by a noise or agitated by something indiscernible to me, had spilled me. I had felt a vague premonition, however, when I treated him to grass and lumps of sugar that morning. He was unusually irritated or excited. I looked at his eyes to learn why but couldn't read his mind. Soon afterward, while I was cantering the horse in the riding ground, he suddenly galloped off. Being just a beginner I couldn't adjust to the sudden change of speed. The first vertebra of my lower spine was punctured, and I was put in a corset for three months. I felt drowsy all the while as if confined in a cocoon.

This morning the alarm suddenly woke me from my long inertia. And abruptly a few lines of a well-known Japanese poem sprang to mind.

> *That is Mt Adatara,*
> *That sparkling river*
> *Is the Abukuma – your birthplace*

The Abukuma River, fed by many tributaries, flows into the Bay of Sendai. Mt Adatara, a dormant volcano with a turquoise-blue lake in its crater, rests gracefully beyond the river. Although shaken out of sleep as if thrown off horseback, I still felt drowsy, like a silk scarf floating softly downstream, or like the river's flickering water reflecting the scarlet-tinged maple leaves along its banks.

Usually I depend on something solid, the way trees root to the earth, but in the emergency I had only the reins to hang onto. When I let go of them, however, and was hurled into the air, I felt strangely freed for an instant. Life, I understand, consists of perpetual partings, from familiar scenes and loved ones, or even from a belief. And yet I would surely want to go home like a stray child if I were utterly lost in an unknown place – say, in space. If you were to go all the way around this planet, you would always get back home. But there's no going back home once you've been born here. You have to go through life, door-to-door, looking for hidden answers.

> *Those white dots*
> *Are the walls*
> *Of your family's* sake *brewery*

I remember the faint aroma of *sake*, mingled with the taste of ginger lollipops, when I opened the heavy wooden sliding door of my grandfather's closed-down brewery. I pried in every nook and niche, looking for my friends who were hiding somewhere in there; 'spying' them was a daily game in my childhood. Years later, the *sake* brewery was sold to a neighbor and transformed into a soybean-packing plant and shop. My parents as well as my grandparents are no more; they are enshrined in our family altar along with other ancestors. The *sake* fragrance of the brewery is long gone, but in my ear still remain echoes of young girls shouting, *'Mō-ii-kai?* (Are you ready?)' *'Mā-da-da-yo* (No, not yet).'

Serpent, Tornado

      Counting the fragments
            in unspoken prayer,
                  I stared at

the broken *raku* tea bowl, fitted to my hands by years of use – a gift to me from a friend who had found it in an antique shop in Kyoto. I could have had it repaired with gold-dust lacquer, which would have added a new aspect of beauty to the bowl. But instead I put the fragments in a wooden box where I had collected broken pieces of stone, glass, tile, amber, shell, bone, wood, cloth, leather, odds and ends, hoping that someday I could piece them all together into an organic collage.

I had failed to shut tightly the hinged glass doors of the cupboard the night before the earthquake, M7.3 on the Richter scale, shook this area at dawn. In my bed I pulled the blanket over my head and stuck out the twenty seconds of violent shaking. Tremendous energy was discharged.

The earth really meant it. Most of the tiles slid down from the roof of my house. Dishes, plates, cups, bowls, glasses in the cupboard fell from the shelves and broke. Pieces of glass flew in all directions. Finally I got up enough nerve to slip out of bed for a cup of hot green tea, but neither tap water nor town gas were available, and above all it was dangerous to walk barefoot in the kitchen.

      The sun was declining
           subdued as if seen through
                  a frosted glass lampshade, as I

walked downtown afterwards – the air was dense with dust and smelt faintly of gas. Enormous energies, released from the collapsed wooden houses, crushed human bodies and crumbled concrete buildings, were rising in a vortex:

> a dark
> serpent, a
> tornado
> a huge
> trumpet
> of
> lily
> support-
> ing
> the
> threat-
> ening
> skies

Dusk was thickening into night when I came back to my room, littered with books and papers and pieces of broken glass, and went to bed.

I had a vivid sensation that my body was falling apart. I was aware that I was in a dream, but I repeated frantically, '*namu-amida, namu-amida*', calling for help from Amitabha, the Buddha of Infinite Light. I feared if I stopped chanting, my body wouldn't stay in one piece, so I kept on until I felt safe and whole.

Toward daybreak I wake up and go into the kitchen, where the rich perfume of white lilies emanating from the broken crystal vase brings me to my senses.

Renovation

The first day: dishes, plates, cups and glasses were taken from the cupboard, pots and pans from the shelves, and put in cartons. The drawers, closets and chests were cleared of silverware, lacquered bowls, chopsticks and trays. Fragile wine glasses and sake cups were wrapped carefully in soft paper. The old sink unit and the gas stove were removed. The kitchen was stripped of its curtains, the table and chairs carried out in preparation for the renovation of the old wooden house – have you seen my jewels, by the way, my rings, bracelets, necklaces… my accessories?

The second day: They took away the walls and ripped down the ceilings. The girders and crossbeams were revealed. The boards were torn up from the floors. The wind blew through the house, whirling up dust. The skeleton of my home rattled. I felt a chill run down my spine – where are my cosmetics and clothing… and my flower perfumes?

The third day: It was snowing. I went down to the basement to put away old furniture, a cradle, a baby bathtub, a buggy, my son's climbing gear, PCs and text books no longer in use, and then sorted out manuscripts and letters stuffed in a worn-out trunk. I dug out old poems and browsed through them one by one the whole day –

> A voice reverberates
>   from the walls of a cavern
>   hidden from sight
>
> penetrates the mind
>   without vibrating
>   the eardrums –

I was thrown off my guard when I came across the following lines a poet-friend had sent me:

the monk leaves and shuts the door to the cave. i am alone on the cold stone floor, with the sun gone down and my thoughts careening off the blackened walls. what can you say about a night full of stars? what can you say about a lake that blue?

in thirty minutes the monk returns and opens the iron-bound door – i have never felt such silence. i stand and step outside, into a cutting wind. it is the ninth century, the lake has frozen over, and the first star has opened in the sky.

      An image of the Buddha
          wearing only a piece of cloth;
              the eye in the forehead
                    gleams through dust.

Woman in a Blue Robe

Who are you?
Why are you here?
Where are you from?
Who are your parents?
May I have your name, Ma'am?

Do I have to answer all of your questions right now when I'm totally occupied with finding a trash can? Don't be disturbed by my apparition, noble Monk. I have no intention of distracting you from performing the ceremony. I've been going through a list of my own names I want to discard. I don't need a personal name any longer.

Once I was called 'Princess Light' and was loved dearly by my own brother. People used to say my beauty shone through the layers of brocades – as if sunlight were filtering through all shades of yellow and scarlet maple leaves. Our names became the talk of the townspeople, and the rumor drove us to a bare mountain. Among rocks and stumps of trees, the cold steel piercing each other flashed like lightning.

Some hundreds of years before this incident two young men wanted to marry me. In those days I was called 'Blossoming Maid' as I was just arriving at puberty. Taking up swords and bows and arrows, the two youths fought for my sake. My heart was broken. I preferred my own death to theirs. They followed me soon after. Three tumuli in a row were built by the grieving families, mine in the middle. Buried with me were earrings of gold and necklaces of blue beads, as well as bronze mirrors imported from China.

Many times I exchanged love poems in courtship, and on several occasions told fancy stories. One time I even set fire to my parents' house to win back a boyfriend's attention. Another time I went berserk when I found my husband had taken a mistress. Out of jealousy I changed into a column of fire, a female demon, a snake in pursuit of the one who had deserted me. Each time I was called by a different name.

Earth rotates throughout summer, autumn, winter, spring – a simple cell grows into complex life, evolving into all forms and sizes, and then decomposes into elements, cycling through dark and intricate passages between life and death, over and over again. I no longer see flowers, nor smell incense, nor taste liquor, nor feel a caressing touch, but only hear the vibrations of light flowing over my transparent skin.

Pray for me, my dear Monk. Tonight the full moon, multiplied in the flooded paddies before rice-planting, shines alone in the deep sky. I'm wearing only a blue kimono, which is enough for me to live in.

Sole Desire

Composed after seeing an exhibition of the French tapestries, 'The Lady and the Unicorn,' and visiting the White Heron Castle in Himeji, Japan.

> After walking through
> a flurry of falling petals
> our eyes point to one end –
> a dewdrop on a cabbage leaf –

Her hand touching the trunk of a full-blown cherry tree, the child smiled at me in front of the stone wall. As my camera zoomed in, the soaring tower of the castle went out of frame – and out of space-time. Superimposed on the five-year-old girl was a nineteen-year-old princess, who had fled from the burning castle where her husband and her mother-in-law had taken their lives upon suffering complete defeat. And into another castle for help.

It had been her joy to follow petals fluttering in the wind, extending her hands in high spirits. But before her first period, a child marriage was arranged for her, while she was still playing with dolls, adorned with artificial flowers, surrounded by animals on leashes and birds in cages, with a gentle lion and a loyal unicorn to protect her from external enemies. Before her first period, before the curtain was raised, before she knew what was really going to happen. About her own inmost desire nobody cared.

Her lion carried her out of the burning castle, her unicorn single-mindedly attended her – but again she was ordained to appear on another stage, to remarry for political reasons. But this time she had her own choice. What is your sole desire, my lady? She caressed the lion's mane and softly held the unicorn's horn, rocking the beasts to calm them down with her music. Her pet monkey licked the tears on her palm. A white heron circled over her head. Her resolution was firm. This time she refused to obey the order.

'Is this the whole story you wanted to tell me, grandma?'
'Yes, she followed her heart while wars went on.'

'But grandma,' the child retorted, attracted to the merry-go-round in the adjacent park, 'was she happy in the end?'

Well, illness deprived her of her loved family. She cast off her old habits of looking up to the sky and craving freedom from fear of ghosts. Instead, she found consolation in solitude, discarding heavily embroidered clothes, jewels and courtly customs, choosing instead to be canopied with flowering branches of cherry trees. She entered her room, which was empty of all furniture except a circular silver mirror, and rolled up the bamboo blind – there she searched for herself deep down in her reflection.

NOTES & ACKNOWLEDGEMENTS

Notes

OFFERING TO THE BLUE SKY: The word *mawatte* means 'turn' in Japanese. In the Japanese tea ceremony, one turns a bowl of tea three times before bringing it to one's lips or offering it to a deity.

IN PURSUIT OF A BIRD: The italicized section is translated by the author from the *Kojiki*, the oldest collection of songs and stories concerning the founding of Japan and the beginnings of Japanese culture, compiled in the eighth century.

LINKED VERSE WITH SAIGYŌ: The lines by the Buddhist priest-poet Saigyō (1118–1190) are from Burton Watson's *Saigyo, Poems of a Mountain Home* (Columbia University Press, 1991).

SLEEPING TIGER: Saigyō composed this waka (a 31-syllable poem, here translated by the author) on his second trip (1186) to Hiraizumi in the Province of Mutsu (present day Iwate Prefecture in the northernmost part of the mainland of Japan); his purpose was to raise funds for the rebuilding of the Tōdaiji Temple in Nara, which had been burnt down in 1180 during the battle between the Taira and Minamoto clans. Bashō (1644–1694) composed the haiku at the end of the piece when he took the same route as Saigyō on his second homecoming (1676) to Ueno in the Province of Iga (present day Mie Prefecture).

FLOWER ARRANGEMENT: 菜の花や 月は東に 日は西に (*nanohana ya, tsuki wa higashi ni, hi wa nishi ni*). A haiku by Yosa no Buson (1716–1783), who was also a distinguished painter of the Edo period.

SPRING OF LIFE: A magical door, a *dokodemo* door, is one of numerous 'secret devices' in a serial manga for children, *Doraemon*, by Fujiko F. Fujio.

MISSING PIECE OF THE PUZZLE: The lama's words are taken (slightly changed) from the detective novel, *Beautiful Ghosts*, by Eliot Pattison.

HIDE-AND-SEEK: The lines in italics are translated by the author from 'Chieko-shō (Odes for Chieko)' by the sculptor and poet, Kōtarō Takamura (1883–1956).

RENOVATION: The italicized sections are from 'first meditation lessons' in *ex-violinist in kathmandu*, by James C. Hopkins.

WOMAN IN A BLUE ROBE: The anonymous woman is recorded in the Tōdaiji Temple's register of the dead who contributed to or were closely connected with the construction, restoration and maintenance of the temple from the time of its establishment in AD 745. Most of them are emperors, peers, shōguns, daimyōs, high priests, etc. Very few women are registered, but 'a woman in a blue robe' is recorded as the eighteenth name after Minamoto-no-Yoritomo (d. 1199), the founder of the Kamakura shōgunate. During the *o-mizutori* (water-drawing) ceremonies of the Tōdaiji Temple the names in the register are read aloud by a monk to appease the souls of the dead. Sometime during the Shōgen era (1207–1211), when a monk called Jukei was reciting the names in the register, a beautiful woman in a blue robe appeared and asked him, 'Why haven't you read my name?' She looked very sad. The monk was disturbed to see her, but quickly called out 'a woman in a blue robe' and the woman smiled contentedly and disappeared. Since then her 'name' has been recited along with the names of the other benefactors.

SOLE DESIRE: This piece was inspired by the sixteenth-century French tapestries, *The Lady and the Unicorn*, and the story of a

Japanese princess, Senhime (1597–1666), daughter of the third Tokugawa shōgun. She was given in a politically arranged child marriage to the last lord of the Toyotomi, who committed *seppuku* upon defeat in the battle for power between the Tokugawa and the Toyotomi clans. She was rescued from the flames of Osaka Castle and re-married, this time by her own choice, the son of the lord of Himeji Castle, known for its beauty as the White Heron Castle. After losing to illness both her second husband and her small son, she became a nun.

Acknowledgements

The author gratefully acknowledges the editors and publishers of the following journals and books, both online and in print, in which earlier versions of many of these poems first appeared: *aglimpse of, Innisfree Journal, Poetry Kanto, PoetryMagazine.com, Shampoo, Truck, Yomimono*, the anthology *fourW twenty-four*, and the *Poetry & Prose Series* 2015 (Silver Birch Press).

'Linked Verse with Saigyō' was first published (as 'Linked Verse') in *Salutations: A Festschrift for Burton Watson* (Ahadada/ Eleksographia, 2015).

My heartfelt gratitude goes to Doris G. Bargen and James C. Hopkins, who helped me revise some of the poems. I would also wish to give my special thanks to Paul Rossiter whose insightful comments greatly helped me edit the poems for this book.

The pattern on the front cover was drawn by Yasuha Nagasawa; the author photograph is by Doris G. Bargen.

www.ingramcontent.com/pod-product-compliance
Lightning Source LLC
Chambersburg PA
CBHW031215090426
42736CB00009B/926